SAINTS
FOR GIRLS

Written by Solveig Muus and Dan Tesoriero
Illustrations by Michael Adams

TABLE OF CONTENTS

Library of Congress Control Number: 2011919878
ISBN 1-936020-58-4

Artwork and Text © 2010 Aquinas Kids, Phoenix, Arizona.
Second Printing, January 2012

SAINT ANNE

Feast Day: July 26
Patroness of Grandmothers

Tradition tells us that Joachim and Anne, of the royal house of David, had no children, which made them very sad. They trusted in God and devoted themselves to prayer and good works. At the appointed time, God heard their prayers and favored Saint Anne, and she conceived in her womb a daughter, Mary, who would one day become the mother of Jesus.

When Mary was born, her mother Anne began a new life. She watched every movement of her little girl with reverent tenderness, and felt herself deeply blessed by the presence of her immaculate child. Anne and Joachim's home was filled with peace and grace.

Anne was a strong and good woman, and after Jesus was born, she became a grandmother and had many opportunities to be with her daughter and grandson, Jesus. In Hebrew, the name Anne means, "Full of Grace."

She humbly adored God and His Will, and began again to watch and pray, until God called her to unending rest in the home of Mary's Child.

THE BLESSED VIRGIN MARY

Feast Day: September 8

Mother of God

The Virgin Mary is the most beautiful, lovely, and loving of all God's creations. Through God's amazing favor and grace, Mary was conceived in her mother's womb without Original Sin, with which all of us are born. Mary in turn gave her whole self and life to God with all her heart.

God sent the angel Gabriel to Mary when she was a young teenager. Gabriel asked her if she would be willing to become the Mother of Jesus, the Savior of the world. Mary said, "Yes! I am the handmaid of the Lord. Let it be done unto me according to thy word." Joseph, to whom she was engaged, took Mary as his wife, and Jesus was born.

Mary cared for Jesus and Joseph with all the love in her heart. She got up before dawn to prepare breakfast, and worked very hard all day cooking, cleaning, spinning, sewing, laundering, and going to the well for water!

Mary was with Jesus when He was born in the stable and she was with Him when He died on the cross for our sins. Before He died, Jesus gave us Mary to be our Mother as well. When Mary's life was over, God took her into heaven, and crowned her Queen of Heaven and Earth!

SAINT LUCY

Feast Day: December 13

Patroness of Eyesight

Saint Lucy is a greatly beloved third century Italian martyr. Her mother suffered for many years from a blood disease. When help could not be found, Lucy told her mother the story of the woman in the Bible who had been healed of her illness when she touched the hem of Jesus' robe. Lucy told her mother to touch the tomb of Saint Agatha, and that if she did this, her mother would be healed.

Lucy and her mother went to Saint Agatha's tomb. They touched it and prayed all night, before falling asleep. Saint Agatha appeared to Lucy while she slept, and called her "Sister." She revealed that Lucy's mother would be healed and that Lucy herself would one day give her life for Our Lord. Lucy's mother was healed instantly, and she allowed Lucy to give her wealth to the poor and to consecrate her virginity to Christ.

A young man to whom Lucy had been promised in marriage accused her as a Christian, and the Roman governor had her eyes gouged out. God miraculously restored Lucy's eyesight, and the governor then set her on fire. Again, God saved her. Finally, Lucy was martyred with a dagger. She was true to her dear Jesus to the end.

SAINT BARBARA

Feast Day: December 4

Patroness of Builders and Protection from Storms

Barbara was born the daughter of a pagan father during the reign of the Roman Emperor Maximilian. Barbara's father presented her with many young men who wanted to marry her, but she refused them all. This made Barbara's father very angry, so he built a high tower and threw her into it as a punishment.

Barbara spent her time in the lonely tower praying and studying the Scriptures to learn about Jesus. One day, when her father was away, she was secretly baptized. Then she had three windows built into her tower, to remind her of the Trinity: God the Father, Son, and Holy Spirit.

When her father found out that Barbara had become a Catholic he was very angry and he tried to kill her, but God saved her. Her father then took her to a judge who had her punished. Barbara held on to her faith in Jesus, and in a rage, her father took her up a mountain and cut off her head while she was saying her prayers. On the way down, he was himself stuck by a flash of lightning and died. Saint Barbara is the Patron Saint for Protection from lightning and storms, a sure helper from heaven.

SAINT CATHERINE OF SIENA

Feast Day: April 29

Patroness of Purity

Catherine of Siena was born the daughter of humble Italian weavers in 1347. As a child, she loved to pray and even had visions of angels. Catherine made a vow to remain a virgin for Christ. At the age of 15, she entered the Third Order of Saint Dominic. Catherine remained in her father's shop, where she served people with love and joy every day. At home, Catherine prayed much and enjoyed God's presence and His love.

After some time, Our Lord told Catherine to travel through Italy and to bring His people back to obedience to the Pope. Through her love and teaching, God brought many people close to His Son Jesus and the Catholic faith. Through Catherine's prayers and work, Pope Gregory XI returned from France to Rome, and she encouraged him to help bring peace to the people of Italy.

God gave Catherine many spiritual gifts. She worked miracles and guided many people through her words and deeds. Catherine died at the age of 33. On October 4, 1970, Pope Paul VI declared Saint Catherine of Siena to be a Doctor, or True Teacher, of the Church.

SAINT JOAN OF ARC

Feast Day: May 30

Patroness of Servicewomen

On January 6, 1412, Joan of Arc was born in France. At a very early age, she heard the voices of saints, who spoke to her about God. Then one day, her voices of Saint Michael, Saint Catherine, and Saint Margaret told Joan to go to King Charles VII of France and help him fight his enemies. At that time the English king and other dukes wanted to gain the throne of France for themselves.

After overcoming many difficulties, 17-year-old Joan wondrously won the battle for Orleans, France, with a small army. She won many more battles, and helped King Charles to regain the throne of France.

The enemies of France kidnapped Joan and threw her into prison. They then tricked her into saying things that made her look like a heretic. Joan was condemned to death because she refused to lie and say the saints had not spoken to her. She was burned at the stake on May 30, 1431, at the age of 19. However, the Church later recognized Joan's faith in God and her obedience to Him, and she was canonized as Saint Joan of Arc.

SAINT RITA

Feast Day: May 22
Patroness of Impossible or Lost Causes

Saint Rita was born in Italy in 1381. She wanted to devote her life to God and become a nun, but her parents arranged for her to marry the town watchman, a man named Mancini. Rita obediently married him and bore twin sons, but sadly, he had a violent temper.

After 18 years of marriage, Mancini was stabbed to death by an enemy, but he repented on his deathbed, thanks to Rita's prayers. After some delay, Rita was admitted to the convent of Saint Magdalen at age 36. She lived 40 years in the convent, in great prayer and charity, working for peace in the area.

Rita had a great devotion to the Passion of Christ. She loved Jesus especially for all He had suffered to save us. One day as she knelt in prayer, her forehead was miraculously pierced by a thorn from the Crown of Thorns.

After suffering 15 years, Saint Rita died of tuberculosis on May 22, 1457. Saint Rita knows what it is like to be a wife, a mother, a widow, and a nun. She can pray for us when we are in very difficult situations.

SAINT CLARE

Feast Day: August 11
Patroness of Television

As a young girl, Clare helped her mother care for the poor people of Assisi. Inspired by the preaching of Saint Francis, Clare gave her life to Jesus at the age of 19. She asked Saint Francis to cut off her beautiful hair and to give her the Franciscan habit. Clare founded the Poor Clares, who wore no shoes, ate no meat, lived in a poor house, and kept silent. Yet they were very happy, because Our Lord was close to them all the time.

In 1244, enemy soldiers came to attack the Poor Clare convent in Assisi. Although very sick, Clare had her sisters carry her to the wall, where she placed a monstrance containing the Blessed Sacrament. As the enemies came closer, Clare begged God for help. A child's voice answered, "I will keep you always in My care." Suddenly a great fear struck the attackers, and they fled for their lives! Saint Clare helped Saint Francis with his new order. One day, since she was too ill to attend Mass, an image of the service appeared on her cell wall – and that is why she is the patroness of television! Clare died in 1253, and the pope canonized her two years later. Today her body lies incorrupt in the church of Santa Chiara in Assisi.

SAINT ROSE OF LIMA

Feast Day: August 23
Patroness of Florists

Isabel Flores de Oliva was born in Lima, Peru, in 1586. She was so lovely that her parents called her Rose. Rose became more beautiful as she grew up, and more in love with Jesus, especially in His presence in the Blessed Sacrament.

Rose worked hard to support her poor parents, who wanted her to marry. Rose, however, chose to live a simple life of prayer and penance. She joined the Dominican Third Order in 1606, at age 20, and gave herself as a virgin to Christ. She lived alone in the family garden, raising vegetables and serving the poor and sick.

God gave Rose visions and blessings, and she also suffered in her body, soul, and spirit. Even so she would pray, "Lord, increase my sufferings, and with them increase Your love in my heart." Jesus continued to grow and shine His presence through Rose to those around her.

One day pirates attacked the city of Lima, but Rose and the people defeated the enemy by prayer before the Blessed Sacrament. Saint Rose of Lima died at age 31.

SAINT MARGARET MARY ALACOQUE

Feast Day: October 17

Patroness of the Sacred Heart

Saint Margaret Mary was born on July 22 in France. Her father died when she was only eight years old, and Margaret Mary became ill with a fever that crippled her. During that time, God gave Margaret a deep love for Jesus in the Blessed Sacrament. After promising to give her life to Jesus, she was cured by the Blessed Virgin Mary and she became a nun.

Jesus appeared to Sister Margaret Mary with His Sacred Heart. The flames coming forth from Jesus' Heart remind us of His burning love for us and His desire that we love Him in return. Jesus revealed to Margaret Mary that He had chosen her to spread devotion to His Sacred Heart.

Jesus said, "Behold this Heart which has loved people so much, and yet they do not want to love Me in return. Through you My divine Heart wishes to spread Its love everywhere on earth."

Sister Margaret Mary obeyed Jesus and devotion to the Sacred Heart of Jesus spread throughout the world. Saint Margaret Mary died in 1690, and was canonized a saint in 1920.

BLESSED KATERI TEKAKWITHA

Feast Day: July 14
Lily of the Mohawks
Co-Patroness of Environment and Ecology

Tekakwitha—She who bumps into things—was born to a Mohawk warrior and a Christian mother in New York in 1656. Tekakwitha's parents died in a smallpox epidemic that left her with weakened eyes and a scarred face.

Tekakwitha was living with her uncle and aunt when the Jesuit priests—the "Blackrobes"— came to her village. Although her family disapproved, she told the priests she wanted to be a Christian, and on Easter Sunday, 1676, she was baptized as Kateri (Catherine) Tekakwitha.

Kateri escaped from her family by journeying many miles to Sault Sainte Marie, Canada, where she found refuge at the Saint Francis Xavier Mission. She received her first Holy Communion there on Christmas Day, 1677, as her poor eyes shone with the light of Jesus. Kateri kindly cared for children, the sick, and the elderly. She spent long hours in prayer and penance.

After a long illness, Kateri died on April 17, 1680. In 1980, Pope John Paul II beatified Kateri Tekakwitha as the first Native American to be declared Blessed.

SAINT ELIZABETH ANN SETON

Feast Day: January 4

Patroness of Converts

Elizabeth Bayley Seton was born into an influential Episcopalian family in 1774. Her early life was quiet, simple, and often lonely. As she grew older, the Bible became her continual instruction, support, and comfort.

In 1794, Elizabeth married William Seton, a wealthy young businessman, but tragically, William died a few years later, leaving Elizabeth a widow at 29 with their five children. Elizabeth felt herself drawn to the Real Presence of Christ in the Eucharist, and she became a Roman Catholic in 1805.

In 1808, Archbishop John Carroll of Baltimore invited Elizabeth to open the first free Catholic school for girls. She did so, and thus began the parochial school system in America. In 1809, Elizabeth founded the Sisters of Charity, establishing orphanages and another school.

Mother Elizabeth Ann Seton died in 1821, only 16 years after becoming a Catholic. On September 14, 1975, the first native-born American to be canonized was Saint Elizabeth Ann Seton!

SAINT FRANCES CABRINI

Feast Day: November 13
Patroness of Immigrants

Frances Xavier Cabrini was born in Italy in 1850. She had 12 brothers and sisters. When she was 18, she wanted to become a nun, but she was too sick to do so. She worked on her parents' farm for many years, until they died.

One day a priest asked Frances to teach in a girls' school. She liked it so much that she founded the Missionary Sisters of the Sacred Heart to care for poor children in schools and hospitals. In 1889, at the urging of Pope Leo XIII, Mother Cabrini came with six nuns to the United States to work among the Italian immigrants.

Filled with a deep trust in God and gifted with a wonderful ability to get things done, Mother Cabrini founded schools, hospitals, and orphanages to help the Italian immigrants and children in America. When Mother Cabrini died in Chicago, Illinois, on December 22, 1917, her institute numbered houses in England, France, Spain, the United States, and South America.

In 1946, Pope Pius XII canonized Mother Frances Xavier Cabrini as the first American citizen to become a saint!

SAINT BERNADETTE SOUBIROUS

Feast Day: April 16

Patroness of the Sick

Bernadette Soubirous was born to a poor family in Lourdes, France, on January 7, 1844. Her family lived in a small dark cottage that had once been a jail! Bernadette was often sick and had a hard time at school. One day she went to gather firewood. Suddenly, in a cave beside a river, she saw a beautiful Lady wearing a blue and white dress and floating above a rose bush. The Lady smiled at Bernadette and made the sign of the cross with a golden rosary. Bernadette knelt down and began to pray.

Crowds began to follow Bernadette to the cave as the Virgin Mary's visits continued. Our Lady asked Bernadette to dig at a spot near the grotto, and suddenly a fresh cool spring of healing waters began to flow. Mary asked Bernadette to have a chapel built by the spot, so people could come there to wash and drink. The water from this spring continues to bring healings to many people.

Bernadette became a nun, and died from tuberculosis when she was only 35 years old. Each year more than five million people come to Lourdes. Pope Pius XI canonized Saint Bernadette in 1933, and to this day, her body remains as beautiful and fresh as it was when she died!

SAINT THERESE OF LISIEUX

Feast Day: October 1

Patroness of the Missions

Therese Martin was born in France in 1873, the youngest of five daughters. She was a happy child who loved Jesus. Her beloved mother died when Therese was still young. A few months later, Therese became so ill with a fever that people thought she was dying. She prayed to Mary, whose statue was in her room. Therese saw Mary smile at her and suddenly she was cured!

Two of Therese's sisters had entered the Carmelite convent, and when she was 15, the bishop gave his permission for Therese herself to enter the convent. Theresa spent her life saving souls, praying, helping priests, sacrificing, and suffering. Loving and trusting in God, as a child, was her "little way" to Jesus. Her favorite saying was, "Love is repaid by love alone."

Therese died at the age of 24, whispering, "My God, I love You!" She wrote, "I will return. I want to spend my heaven doing good on earth." Pope Pius XI canonized Saint Therese in 1925. In 1927 he proclaimed her, along with Saint Francis Xavier, as co-patron of all foreign missions.

On October 17, 1997, Saint Therese of Lisieux was named a Doctor of the Church by Pope John Paul II.

THANK YOU, DEAR GOD!

Dear God, thank You for giving me the gift of life. I like being alive! Thank You for the gift of my Baptism, for giving me new life in Jesus as Your child. Thank You, dear Heavenly Father, for inviting me to know You, to love You, and to serve You.

Thank You for my family, friends, and teachers who help me grow to be a kind and good person. Thank You for Your Saints, my heavenly family, who show me by their lives how to live a life pleasing to You. They received Your love and grace, and loved and served others in return.

May I come to know the Saints and to be filled with their joy. Fill me with Your Holy Spirit, that I may also become holy by loving You, others, and myself. In Jesus' name I pray. Amen.

Dear Mother Mary, Queen of all Saints, pray for us!